USHERING IN
REVIVAL
AND
AWAKENING

USHERING IN
REVIVAL
AND
AWAKENING

BY PAMELA BOLTON

USHERING IN REVIVAL AND AWAKENING

CONTENTS

DEDICATION

First and foremost, I want to thank and dedicate this book to my Lord and Savior, Jesus Christ, who has forgiven me for many sins and shortcomings and who has made all things brand new in my life. You are my First Love.

I also want to thank my mother, Barbara Griffin, for giving me life and for her love and support; and I would like to thank God for blessing me with four precious sons: Alex Merriman, Brandon Merriman, Samuel Merriman, and Caleb Bolton. You will never know on this side of eternity how much you all mean to me. I also want to thank Bill for helping me to get this book published. I can't thank you enough! Each one of you have been a part of my happiest days on Earth. I love you all very much!

This book is also written in loving memory of my brother, Stephen Hannon, who is now cheering us on from Heaven in the great cloud of witnesses.

There are many other people who have sown into my life, and I have listed some of them in the ACKNOWLEDGMENTS at the end of this book.

FOREWORD

DEAN BRAXTON

Ushering in Revival and Awakening is a book that fits right in line with what our Heavenly Father wants on Earth. Just like the verse in Matthew 6:10 states: "Thy Kingdom come, Thy will be done in earth, as it is in heaven (KJV)." There are no divisions in Heaven, and God wants unity in His Church on Earth as well.

As I read this book and took in stories of the movement of God in New York and Vermont areas of the United States of America, I could see how the churches in that region put aside their differences and let God move in their communities. I could not help but think to myself, "If a community of churches did it before with God's help, it can happen again."

Pastor Pamela Bolton put in the time and effort to tell, teach, and explain what took place to bring in revival and awakening to the church at that time and what it is going to take now to bring a revival and awakening at this time and age. She wants the reader to not only walk away with knowledge but to have an experience of God's movements both then and now!

As a writer of many books myself, I appreciate the pure delivery of the history of what took place in *Ushering in Revival and Awakening*. It makes you want to research whether there was a movement of God in your town, city, or county in the past that needs to be discovered again and brought into the light. It makes you wonder if the local churches in your geographical area knew of the history of how God moved in the past if they would come together and lift up the name of Jesus as one church again. As I said at the beginning of this statement, God of all Creation wants His will to be done on Earth as it is in Heaven. So, you will find in reading this book that He wants not only a movement in your location and churches but also a greater outpouring than has ever happened before.

INTRODUCTION

Jesus prayed, *"Thy kingdom come, Thy will be done in earth, as it is in heaven." Matthew 6:10 (KJV)*

"A revival, then, really means days of Heaven upon Earth. "
D. Martyn Lloyd-Jones[1]

If your church were to move into full-blown revival and awakening tomorrow, would you be ready for it? Would you have time in your busy life to fit it in? I believe that right now the Lord is saying to His church, "Now is the time for preparation." We have each been placed here on this planet, not by accident, but by God's design... FOR SUCH A TIME AS THIS. God is moving among His people, and He desires to move in an even more powerful way than He has in the past.

Do you have a passion for more of God in your life, and a hunger and thirst to know Him better? He is our Heavenly Father, and He wants to reveal Himself to each one of us in greater measure so that we can walk more closely with Him and go out and reach those who don't know Jesus Christ as Lord and Savior.

There have been many, many great men and women of God who plowed the ground ahead of us. Some of them include: Smith Wigglesworth, Lester Sumrall, William Booth, Father Ralph DiOrio, John G. Lake, Amy Semple McPherson, Dwight L. Moody, Katherine Khulman, Charles Finney, Maria Woodworth-Etter, John Osteen, John and Charles Wesley, William Seymour, Kenneth Hagin, and Oral Roberts. I would strongly encourage you to read their stories, watch their messages on YouTube, and be blessed by their testimonies of faith. Their lives are examples to us of what God can do with people who are fully surrendered to Jesus.

I believe that right now God wants His people to dig into local, historic wells of revival in their regions in order to bring forth a fresh river of His living water in their cities, towns, and villages again. There are many of you who are reading this book who have prayed for revival and awakening for years, those of you who have broken up the fallow ground in your communities, those who have planted seeds so that your area is ready for a move of God such as the world has never seen.

Our country desperately needs a touch from the Living God to heal our land. Wherever we look, we see division, tension, and strife. We see brokenness all around us. It doesn't matter what community we live in or what our social status is. It's everywhere. We're living in perilous times, and we need a mighty move of God unlike any before.

Today, I know that He is looking for a people who are hungry and thirsty for more of Him. He is looking for those who are passionate about having a relationship with Him. He's looking for those who want Him above all else, those who are willing to die to self and live for Him, no matter what the cost.

John Wesley said, "Give me one hundred preachers who fear nothing but sin and desire nothing but God, and I care not whether they be clergymen or laymen, they alone will shake the gates of Hell and set up the kingdom of Heaven upon Earth."

Acts 4:13 says, *Now when they saw the boldness of Peter and John, and perceived that they were uneducated and untrained men, they marveled.* ***And they realized that they had been with Jesus***. (NKJV)

These men were "ordinary" fishermen with no formal religious training, yet they received the highest of compliments. You might be an "ordinary" person without any formal Bible training. God wants to use you to reach the lost in the area right where you are. You are on the mission field 24/7, in your home, at your workplace, and in your neighborhood.

God is watching for, waiting for, looking for a people who have been with Him, those who are willing to spend quality and quantity time with Him. He is raising up an army of those who love Him to go out and preach the Gospel to the poor, to release those in darkness, and to set captives free. He is looking for those who are willing.

So, I want to ask you, "Why not you? Why not me? Why not right now in our communities?"

In this book, we're going to discuss some things that we can do as the church of Jesus Christ to position ourselves to help usher in revival and spiritual awakening in our local neighborhoods. I pray that as you read this, you will be encouraged, challenged, and blessed.

CHAPTER 1

BECOMING INTENTIONALLY UNCONVENTIONAL

JUNE 8, 2019
PRAYER MEETING AT THE OLD BRICK CHURCH IN WHITEHALL, NY

When I finally stood up, I looked out at the people; I thought to myself, "How did we get here? This is the answer to so many prayers, some even prayed two-hundred years ago. God is so pleased with this!"

It was overwhelming, and I had to hold back tears of joy as I realized that we were not only watching history in the making, but we were a part of it... history that made a mark for all of eternity. What an overwhelming thought!

For some other pastors and men and women of God in our area, it was what they had desired for years too. There were many believers, including pastors, from different denominations and churches from all over our region, all worshiping God together in unity. It was so wonderful to finally see people coming together for Jesus and Him alone. They didn't come with their own agendas but solely to praise, worship, and pray in one accord.

Later in this book, I will share the rest of this story with you, but for now, I am going to share with you how our ministry began.

OUT OF THE BOX WORSHIP CENTER – OUR STORY

For far too long, we have built nice, neat boxes for God, and we like to keep Him inside of these theological and doctrinal boxes, because this makes us feel secure. We have also built boxes around ourselves that keep us from being all that we are called to be for God's glory. We have to purpose in our hearts to become intentionally unconventional regarding the things of God... to be open to what He's telling us to do right now. At the same time, we do recognize that there are some foundational truths relating to Salvation that cannot be compromised. For example: Jesus was, and is, and always will be God.

We also believe that ministries should be under a church covering, and we encourage every believer to be a part of a local fellowship of believers who teach God's Word and hold one another accountable in love. We also believe a strong Biblical grounding is needed to mature believers for the work of the ministry as found in Ephesians 4.

In July of 2013, Out of the Box Worship Center, our local storefront ministry, was formed to be a place to bring the people of God together to seek Him and to connect with unsaved and hurting people in our community. We have a heart to reach people who have been hurt in the church or who might feel uncomfortable walking through the doors of a traditional church building. Some are struggling with feelings of guilt for things that they have done in the past or over things that were done to them by others. Some have a fear of not measuring up, and still others think that they don't have appropriate clothing to wear to attend services. In the past, I've heard all of these explanations and more.

We decided that we needed to become intentionally unconventional. At the time, we knew that we had to change the way that we were trying to reach the local people in our community, because we realized that our old methods weren't very effective.

At Out of the Box, we believe that everyone matters equally to God, and we know that God is pursuing all people with His boundless love! We knew that we needed to do something to reach the lost, hurting, and rejected in our community and that He is far more concerned about what their hearts look like than how they're dressed.

We also believe that it is difficult for small churches and ministries to have all of the five-fold ministry offices in operation in local, small churches. So we try to give opportunity for ministry from all of these offices in order to help those who have been trying to grow and mature spiritually to become true disciples, to be complete in Christ. We want them to walk in the plan that God has for their lives, and we not only want this for the people who come through the doors at Out of the Box but also for you.

We don't claim to have all the answers, but we're trying to do our part, sometimes with just one person at a time. We know that there are other churches in our community that are trying to do their parts as well. And we also know that when we do our part, God will take care of the rest.

Jesus' ministry was "out of the box" and very unconventional, and we want to be more and more like Him every day. It is my prayer that you do too.

I have been told more than once that I am very unconventional. When I first heard this, I wondered, "What exactly does this mean? Should I take this as a compliment or as an insult?"

As I reflected on this choice of a word, I chose to take it as a compliment, because many of the men and women who God has used throughout history have been quite unconventional. Jesus was very unconventional in His ministry style too, and He was the biggest history maker who ever walked on the planet. God is looking for more people who are willing to do church in unconventional ways, while never compromising the Gospel message.

I believe that God gave me the vision for Out of the Box Worship Center some time before it came into existence. I prayed and looked at buildings for over a year before God made it clear which one was His choice. Some of the ways that we have reached out to people include the following: having clown ministry come in, playing praise music out on the sidewalk while having clothing and other giveaways, setting up a small store where everything was free, having clothing racks set up all the time at our newest location, having different musicians and guest speakers come from different denominations, bringing in puppet shows, sharing the Gospel through skits, holding twelve-step groups, having a prayer tent set up in our local park, walking around town and talking to and praying for people, hosting outreach events in our local park, hosting soup and bread luncheons, giving out free Christmas gifts to area children, Christmas caroling, serving hot dogs and chips out on the sidewalk, and many more things as well.

When our friend, Edward Fox, who spent some time in Europe years ago, first saw the space that we rented, he told me that it is not uncommon in Europe for people to hold church meetings in buildings very similar to ours, many of which are rundown and just plain, simple rooms. God has moved powerfully in those places, and many people have come into relationship with Jesus as a result of visiting them.

When I went to Englewood, Chicago, in August of 2019, I saw many storefront churches there as well. They weren't fancy, but the members were doing their best to reach out to the people in their area who are in desperate need.

So, what might REVIVAL and AWAKENING look like in your church today? God is looking for unconventional people who will begin to think "outside the box"; those who are willing to get out of their comfort zones; those who are open to new and creative ways to share the Gospel message; and those who are willing to go out onto the streets and share Jesus with those who don't already know Him, lead them into the Kingdom of God, and then disciple them.

If we don't learn to listen to the Holy Spirit and be Spirit-led people, in greater measure than we already are, we are going to miss the coming move of God that is going to be massive. Revival and awakening aren't going to happen the way that they did years ago. It isn't going to be about one STAR evangelist who people travel miles and miles to hear speak, but it will be about each person who is a part of the Body of Christ being used by God to reach the lost.

God has been preparing men and women for decades for SUCH A TIME AS THIS. He desires to use many people who are unknown but who are willing to be used to bring in the harvest of souls. Not only will He use those who have been quietly being prepared in obscurity, but He will also use those who come into His Kingdom now.

We have tried for years to get new people to come into our churches, and for the most part, we have not been very successful. Many times, when there are guests, they are Christians who are visiting from other churches; or they are looking for a new place to worship, because there was something at their prior church with which they were not happy.

More often, we need to think about things from a heavenly perspective down rather than from an earthly perspective up. What is God saying right now? What does He want to do in this season? What does He want you to do? What does He want your church to do? We know that He wants to do new things in the lives of His people, but sometimes this isn't possible because they are stuck in "religious" ruts. In some churches, there are people who will say that things have to be done a certain way just because that is the way they have always been done.

Since Out of the Box Worship Center came into existence, I can say with confidence that there have been over 500 people who have come through the doors of our humble, storefront ministry, some for a period of time, others for just one visit. Many have been influenced for eternity.

The Bible says that some plant, some sow, and some reap (1 Corinthians 3:6 and John 4:37-38). That is what we have seen at Out of the Box. There are people who have attended and become believers who then moved out of our area or on to a different church. There are those who have been encouraged in their faith, and there are also those who have had opportunity to minister for the first time, like our dear friend, Scott Heller.

In the spring of 2018, Nicole Banta (former missionary to Columbia) and I felt that God was calling us to begin praying throughout our village and to cover every house and business with prayer. We let people know what we were planning to do and invited them to join us, and God brought together a small team. Then we strategically mapped out our plan. Every Friday, we met to pray together for a short time, and then we went out on the streets. You would be surprised at how many people were open to receiving prayer and having us visit with them. At our local, annual town festival, we set up a tent and offered free prayer to anyone who desired it. We also gave away Bibles and other Christian literature as well as provided sand art for the children.

In the summer of 2018, I believe that God impressed upon me to hold a free pastors' dinner for pastors and their spouses. We had a wonderful evening with good food, fellowship, praise and worship, and an inspiring message. We had 25 local leaders in attendance at Historic Grounds, a little restaurant in our village. In the spring of 2019, we held another meeting to bless area pastors. Again, we had about 25 local leaders attend, and people told me afterwards how blessed they were to be able to be there. You just know that God is doing something special when pastors from different church backgrounds are excited about gathering together in unity to honor our Lord and Savior, Jesus Christ.

For over four years, Pastor Jim Peterson from the local First Baptist Church, Father Rendell Torres from Our Lady of Hope Catholic Church, and I have been meeting to pray for our town and each other once a month. God has been building relationships between us, and now we are seeing fruit that is coming forth from these bonds. These prayer times helped lay the groundwork for a special prayer event that we had in Whitehall, NY, on June 8, 2019. I will share the details about this meeting in Chapter 4.

OTHER MINISTRIES THAT ARE "OUT OF THE BOX"

I know of several other churches and ministries that have done and are doing very unconventional outreaches in their communities, and I'm sure that there are many others as well. Here are a few examples:

Cambridge, NY
Living Waters Evangelistic Ministries, founded by Pastors Tim and Cindylee Bohley in 1991, is a ministry with several churches and other outreach ministries, including Jacob's Well Family Worship Center in Cambridge, NY. They

are real people who are trying to serve the Lord the best way that they know how. They are also the covering for Out of the Box Worship Center, and they have been 100 % supportive of our evangelistic endeavors.

Over the years, Living Waters has stepped out and done some unusual and unconventional outreaches. They have opened their doors for puppet shows; coffeehouses; weekend-long, bi-annual tent meetings; clown ministry; inner-city ministry; trainings; dinner events; mission trips to Andros, Bahamas, and West Virginia; dance teams; outreaches in their local park; Seders; and Lydia's Closet–an outreach to the community that had inexpensive clothing and other items as well as live Christian music, Christian books available for reading, Harvest Parties for the children in the community, coffee, and fellowship. The purpose of Lydia's Closet was to help support missions.

Jacob's Well has come alongside other local churches and ministries to support them, and this church has also helped many individuals who have had visions to evangelize. For the past two years, they have hosted the local pastors' prayer meetings twice a month, and sometimes serve the pastors breakfast as well. They have opened their arms to and welcomed many guest ministers and musicians. They also disciple people and encourage them to fulfill their God-given calls, especially those who have visions for evangelism. Their doors have also been open to many other groups in their community that have needed a place to meet.

The Livings Waters' slogan is: "Teach, Preach, and Send."

Granville, NY

Since 2014, Granville Assembly of God church members have been going to their local Price Chopper once a week to pray together and then offer to pray for people in the store. Pastor Bill Steinmetz told me that eighty percent of the people they talk to want to receive prayer. This again just goes to show us that there are many hurting people who are waiting for us, the church, to reach out to them.

Under the guidance of Issa and Cheryl Najjar, Granville AOG spearheaded a ministry called "Lighthouse" in 2013. It is an outreach to children in their community that includes several large events each year, including one in their local park—with skits, games, gifts, prizes, and food. As a result of this ministry, many local people have heard the Gospel message.

Fort Edward, NY

Pastor Derik Bartholomew from Cornerstone Outreach Center caught a vision to help feed the needy when he saw hungry families in his community. His church started out by going to Aldi's and purchasing food using church funds. In the beginning, there were just a couple of families involved, and then the church members began to see how big the need really was. As they reached out, many more people began to come for food.

They had limited space for people to wait for their turn to receive items, and many of them didn't feel comfortable waiting in the church sanctuary. They were afraid that they might make a mess or get things dirty, so the church prayed about how to make things more accessible and welcoming.

The church had pews, and they decided to try to sell them on Craigslist. Amazingly, within a few days, they sold. The church replaced the pews with chairs, and from there, the food ministry began to grow. They were also able to purchase tables so that they could feed people while they waited.

It was difficult to keep up with the needs, but they began to love on people, including volunteers from the community who were not believers. And most importantly, they were able to influence them for Christ.

Their current building isn't large enough for the local need, so they have a building project in progress right now called Cornerstone Dream Center.

Their slogan is: "Building a Cornerstone for a Better Community."

They, like us at Out of the Box, have been going out on the streets and ministering for the past year. In doing so, they have also found many people who are open to receiving prayer, and many have become believers.

Albany, NY

For several years, during the summers on Friday evenings, Mike and Barbara Griffin headed up an outreach ministry under the covering of The Prayer and Healing Center in Albany, NY. When people from both churches that I was connected with at the time (Jacob's Well Family Worship Center in Cambridge, NY, and Faith Chapel Assembly of God in Whitehall, NY) were able to make it, they would go down to Albany to help with this outreach. There was always Christian music, food, games, clowns, prizes, and skits out on the sidewalk in the inner city. People would present the Gospel message in creative ways that would hold the attention of the children, teens, and adults. A big part of the reason that this type of outreach worked in this area was that people were able to develop relationships in a nonthreatening environment. Many lives were impacted for eternity as a result of this "out of the box" style of outreach.

Oak Hill, WV

Reverends Charles and Sharon Miller (precious Methodist pastors) spent several years running Thursday night community prayer events at an old armory that was beautifully restored. This ministry blossomed as they fed people a full meal and then had praise and worship and prayer for their community. Many people were saved, healed, and delivered. People from all different walks of life attended, so they did outreach to the poorest of the poor, and they also ministered to the affluent. There was something for everyone, and many different denominations came together to be part of what God was doing. The ministry grew, and eventually they began holding weekend-long "Awaken Conferences" where people could go and stay and have all of their meals and lodging included (if needed). They would have prayer, teaching, Communion, praise and worship, and preaching throughout the entire weekend, and God moved in power.

Albany, NY

God has given Pastor Charlie Muller many creative, "out of the box" ways to reach people in the inner city of Albany in Arbor Hill. In 1995, he started the J.C. Club Children's Feeding Center that feeds approximately 100 children lunch, seven days a week during the summer. And he has also used things like an ice cream truck that serves free fruit smoothies, provided Christmas presents, and providing fans for people during the hot months. He also created a Dream Center, complete with audiovisual equipment and a kitchen to minister to teens. His current endeavor is building a beautiful home for foster children. Pastor Charlie also founded two churches in the Albany area. God has moved powerfully through this ministry for years as a result of Pastor Charlie being open to Holy Spirit-inspired, creative ideas.

Hillsville, VA

Knowing the vision that I had for our town, Reverend Kevin Richardson (Dean of Academics at the Bible College that I attended) recommended that I go and meet Ronnie Collins, a Methodist pastor who had a vision to reach people in the heart of his community. Pastor Ronnie pastored at a local Methodist Church. At first, not everyone in his congregation was convinced that an outreach ministry/church would work or was even necessary. The storefront church opened their doors during the week and did unconventional ministry. They hung out with people, developed relationships with them, had interesting activities (especially for youth), and shared the Gospel with them.

The name of the ministry was Out of the Box Worship Center. As soon as I heard the name, I loved it; and I was anxious to see what God was doing there. I had heard reports that this church had grown from zero to 300 people in just three, short years.

Pastor Ronnie was happy to meet with my fellow workers and me. He sat down with us and shared the story of how Out of the Box had come to be, how God had moved in power, and that many people had become believers and been baptized. The church grew so quickly that they had to rent an additional storefront that adjoined the one they already had. Later on, when it continued to grow, they had to add another location as well. I asked Pastor Ronnie if it would be okay with him if when we opened the storefront ministry in New York we named it after the work that he was doing in Virginia, and of course he said, "yes."

WHAT ABOUT YOU?

Are you willing to be open to the leading of the Holy Spirit and willing to become intentionally unconventional in order to be about our Father's business? God isn't looking for you to do someone else's part, but He is looking for you to do your own part. If you are willing, He'll show you what to do and how to do it. What you're called to do might look very different from what someone else is doing, depending upon your call and the needs in your community.

CHAPTER 2

REVIVAL
AND
AWAKENING
THE 100-YEAR PROPHECIES

There are several 100-year prophecies from near the year 1900, which state that God is going to pour out His Spirit in a more powerful way than ever before and that we will see worldwide revival and awakening. I believe that we are in the birthing stages of this final outpouring of God's Glory upon Earth.

Pastor Michael Edds wrote the following article, and he gave us permission to share it with you in this book.[1]

Great Spiritual Awakenings have swept the world over the centuries. They have changed lives and the very culture in which we live. An Awakening is a special time when God comes down and saturates a place and a people with His presence. There is a final Great Awakening coming.

The Final Great Awakening–
An Endtime Revival

The great Azusa Street Awakening, which over the years resulted in 600 million being swept into the Kingdom of God and gave birth to the Pentecostal Movement, began in 1906. It was one of the greatest outpourings of the Spirit of God since Pentecost. Multitudes were saved, healed, and filled with the Holy Spirit. Incredible miracles occurred.

This great revival moved from Los Angeles to its new focal point of Chicago, Illinois. The two great centers of revival in Chicago were the North Avenue Mission and the Stone Church. Pentecost swept from Chicago to Canada, Europe, South America, and Africa. One of the greatest outpourings occurred at Stone Church in 1913. The renowned evangelist Maria Woodworth-Etter began a revival on July 2, 1913 at Stone Church.

The services were to last until the end of July but continued for six months. This was a time of divine appointment for the city of Chicago; God rent the heavens and came down!! Scenes from the days of the Early Church began to occur at Stone Church. Word began to spread throughout Chicago of miraculous healings, deliverance from demonic possession, conversions, and of the outpouring of the Holy Spirit happening in these meetings. Advertisement was no longer necessary! The city was incredibly shaken.

Word spread of the miraculous intervention of God. Thousands came on trolleys, buggies, and trains, while many walked. Some came from distances of 1,600 miles away. 1,200 to 1,500 packed into Stone Church each night. The basement was filled, and many stood out on the street. Street meetings were held to accommodate them. Three services were held on Sundays!

As Christians prayed around the altar one evening, Sister Woodworth-Etter and others gave the following powerful prophecy and divine promise, which they prophesied would occur within 100 years of the 1913 Chicago Visitation. She prophesied of this coming End Time Revival....

"We are not yet up to the fullness of the Former Rain and that when the Latter Rain comes, it will far exceed anything we have seen!"

*Rev. William Seymour, the leader of the Azusa Street Awakening, also prophesied that **in 100 years there would be an outpouring of God's Spirit and His Shekinah Glory that would be greater and more far reaching than what was experienced at Azusa.***

It has been almost 100 years since these prophecies were given. In my own beloved church, I am seeing the beginnings of this prophecy being fulfilled.... Healing and miracles are occurring! The anointing of the Holy Spirit on the services is heavy and growing each week. Something IS happening! I believe that we have reached the time of the fulfillment of these 100-year-old prophecies. We must be diligent to pray, intercede, and protect what the Lord is doing. We must encourage and edify one another as never before. We must crucify every critical, judgmental, and religious spirit that may be within us. We must put on the holiness and righteousness of Christ. Our time of divine destiny has come. We are about to experience what Brother Seymour and Sister Woodworth-Etter foresaw. God is about to rend the heavens and come down! The greatest revival in the history of the church is at hand!

Why aren't we seeing the kinds of miracles that took place in the early New Testament Church happening today or at least miracles on the same scale? Have you tried to make sense of it with your own reasoning? We know it is God's heart to heal and to reveal Himself to people. We also know that Jesus promised that we would do even greater works than the works that He did while He was on this planet (John 14:12). The problem is definitely not with God. But what is it?

Sometimes, there are other factors that we aren't completely aware of taking place in the spirit realm. If you don't see a miracle happen that you've been praying for, don't give up. Healings and miracles will take place where people take

God at His Word, allow the Holy Spirit to move, and keep believing.

For many years, I have struggled to figure out what the difference is between the early church and the church today. I have cried out to God to stretch forth His hand and daily perform miracles so that the world will once again see the truth of who He is. I haven't been asking for miracles for the sake of seeing miracles, but so unbelievers would come to know Jesus as Lord and Savior, and believers would be healed, made whole, and fulfill their calls, all for God's Glory.

CHAPTER 3

THREE KEYS TO USHERING IN REVIVAL AND AWAKENING

Over the years, I have come to understand that there are three keys that are crucial to positioning ourselves to receive from and to be used by God. These three are all important, kind of like the legs of a birthing stool. If one is absent, the whole stool will be off balance. If we want to usher in revival and awakening and allow God to birth through us what He desires right now, then we need to be balanced.

1. Walking in UNITY in the LOVE of GOD

There is no "I" in "TEAM," and there are no lone rangers in the Body of Christ.

I have a dream of a day when Christians will no longer be defined by their denomination or where they attend church, but they will be defined by whether or not they are a child of God. It will be a wonderful day when denominational barriers are torn down, and many people who love Jesus will come together for special services and events to worship and praise Him and pray together as one Body.

In John 17:20-23, we read the prayer that Jesus prayed for all believers everywhere, including each one of us: *"I do not pray for these alone, but also for those who will believe in Me through their word; that they all may be one, as You, Father, are in Me, and I in You; that they also may be one in Us, that the world may believe that You sent Me. And the glory which You gave Me I have given them, that they may be one just as We are one: I in them, and You in Me; that they may be made perfect in one, and that the world may know that You have sent Me, and have loved them as You have loved Me."*

It always amazes me when I think about this portion of scripture—to think that 2,000 years ago, Jesus prayed for you and me to walk in unity with Him and with other believers. He could have prayed about so many other things, but this must be very important since it is one of the things that He focused on.

Why is UNITY so important that Jesus prayed it for each one of us? Because it reveals how the world will be drawn to Jesus.... By watching how we who are Christians walk in love—they'll know we are Christians **by our love for one another** (John 13:35).

We have to let go of the denominational and doctrinal differences that separate us and walk in unity as Jesus prayed for us to do. If a belief won't keep us out of Heaven, then it shouldn't separate us from working together for the Kingdom of God while we're here on the planet. We need to respect one another and recognize that differences in Bible interpretation that are not Salvation issues should not separate us.

This doesn't mean that we're advocating for a one-world religion or that we agree with everything that another brother or sister in Christ believes, but that we recognize that people who put their trust in Jesus as Lord and Savior of their lives are part of the family of God. Every one of us will be surprised when we get to Heaven and see just how many things we have believed to be absolutes that weren't quite the way that we thought they were.

God may have people connected in different denominations because He has different calls on both their lives and their churches. If we can recognize this, then we won't feel the need to convince others to become more like us. Our hearts' desire should be that they become more like Jesus and walk in their own call.

Just because someone doesn't worship with the same style of music or have the same style of delivery of the Word that we do, doesn't mean that they are not right with God.

In Mark 9:38-41 it says: *Now John answered Him, saying, "Teacher, we saw someone who does not follow us casting out demons in Your name, and we forbade him because he does not follow us."* (NKJV)

*But Jesus said, "Do not forbid him, for no one who works a miracle in My name can soon afterward speak evil of Me. **For he who is not against us is on our side.** For whoever gives you a cup of water to drink in My name, because you belong to Christ, assuredly, I say to you, he will by no means lose his reward."*

You might say, "But the Bible says, 'Study to shew thyself approved unto God, a workman that needeth not to be ashamed, rightly dividing the word of truth'" (2 Timothy 2:15, KJV). And yes, it does say that. But for many years, we have taken this God-breathed scripture, which is meant to encourage us to know why we believe what we believe, and used it as an excuse for spiritual pride and division. Oh, how this must grieve the heart of God!

He delights when His people dwell together in UNITY.
Psalm 133:1-3 (NKJV)
Behold, how good and how pleasant it is
For brethren to dwell together in unity!

It is like the precious oil upon the head,
Running down on the beard,
The beard of Aaron,
Running down on the edge of his garments.
It is like the dew of Hermon,
Descending upon the mountains of Zion;
For there the LORD commanded the blessing—
Life forevermore.

If we want to be in the place where God commands His life-giving blessing, then we need to walk in unity with our true sisters and brothers in Christ.

2. PRAYER (Personal and Corporate)

*"if **My people** who are **called by My name** will **humble themselves**, and **pray** and **seek My face**, and **turn from their wicked ways**, then **I will hear from heaven**, and will **forgive their sin** and **heal their land**."* 2 Chronicles 7:14 (NKJV)

God is looking for a people who will humbly go before Him in **repentance and with faith-filled prayers, believing that He will do what He said He will do.** If we truly want to hear from Heaven, then it is important for us to pray both individually as well as corporately. There has never been a REVIVAL that has not been preceded by prayer.

1 John 1:9 says: **"If we confess our sins, He is faithful and just to forgive us our sins** and to cleanse us from all unrighteousness." We need to confess our sins and turn from them so that nothing will hinder our prayers, and we will be more fully usable by God. We also need to forgive ourselves and move on, because we have work to do for the Kingdom of God.

Learn to listen to the voice of God in prayer. A revival will come as you follow the leading of the Holy Spirit. Don't just jump out and do something because it's a good idea. Hear from the Father what His will is in Heaven right now, and pray like Jesus did—that Heaven will come to Earth. What is the Father showing you to do right now? Get God's heart through prayer, and be led by the Holy Spirit.

My heart's cry is: "Revive us again, O Lord!"

3. OBEDIENCE (Walking in Holiness)

"If you love Me, keep My commandments." John 14:1 (NKJV)

Obedience is not merely a suggestion; it was commanded by Jesus Himself. Let's ask God to work in each of our hearts, to help us to be more like Jesus each day, and to send us forth into the world to share with people just how much God loves them.

My prayer for each of you is that God will fuel the spark that's already in your heart into a full flame, that you will be set on fire for Jesus, be full of the Holy Spirit and power, and be a bright light to the lost in this world in these last days. If you are already on fire for Jesus, I pray that you will burn even more brightly.

Jesus was our example, and this is how He walked:
*Let this mind be in you, which was also in **Christ Jesus**: Who, being in the form of God, thought it not robbery to be equal with God: **But made himself of no reputation, and took upon him the form of a servant, and was made in the likeness of men**: And being found in fashion as a man, he humbled himself, and became obedient unto death, even the death of the cross. Wherefore God also hath highly exalted him, and given him a name which is above every name: That at the name of Jesus every knee should bow, of things in heaven, and things in earth, and things under the earth; And that every tongue should confess that Jesus Christ is LORD, to the glory of God the Father.* Philippians 2:5-11 (KJV)

We have to be careful not to try to make a reputation for ourselves and to always point people to God.

He who says he abides in Him (Jesus) *ought himself also to walk just as He walked.* 1 John 2:6 (NKJV)

As our friend, Dean Braxton, says, "Everything that God created acts in the manner that it was created to. A tree acts like a tree; a fish acts like a fish; and a Christian ought to act like a Christian! Act like who you are!"

CHAPTER 4

DIGGING UP LOCAL, OLD WELLS OF REVIVAL

OUR STORY
Prayer Service at the Old Brick Church

In August of 2018, I felt that God was impressing me to go to our local Historical Society in Whitehall, NY, to see what I could find out about prior times of revival and awakening in our area. My passion was to find out what God had done in our little community in the past. I knew that He is not a respecter of persons (Acts 10:34), so if He did something for some people in our little town years ago, He'd do it for us, too. I found newspaper clippings about revivals that had taken place long ago in our town. There is one church in particular that I found a lot of information about—The Methodist Episcopal Church (hereafter referred to as the Old Brick Church) in East Whitehall, NY.

During the fall of 2018, I felt that God was directing me to ask to hold a special prayer meeting at this small, old country church that is located just a few miles outside of our village. Currently, there is only one service a year held there, and the church still doesn't have any electricity or running water.

I asked the Old Brick Church board if we could use the property for a one-day prayer event, and after they asked me several questions, they approved our request. I was told by a lifetime resident of our community that we had found favor, but I didn't realize the extent of what that meant until later.

One day, I stopped by the Old Brick Church to thank one of the board members who was working outside on a restoration project. He told me that he couldn't remember a time when that church had allowed ANY group to use that building other than family members or friends for weddings and funerals.

I just knew that God had planned this service; it was to be a special, divine appointment. Over the next several months, we went out to the property and prayed over it numerous times. We were digging up the old wells of revival in our area and petitioning Heaven for fresh Living Water.

On Saturday, June 8, 2019, we had a wonderful prayer service. We were blessed to have at least 17 pastors and 15 different churches in attendance. Denomination wise, we know that there were people from each of following churches as well as several independent churches: Presbyterian, Catholic, Assemblies of God, Lutheran, American Baptist, Southern Baptist, Congregational, and Independent Assemblies of God. The Episcopal and Methodist pastors wanted to attend, but they weren't able to due to prior commitments. We all worshiped and prayed together in unity, and the presence of God was very powerful in the place. We shared about prior revivals in our area as well as others throughout New York State and Vermont.

I looked out and saw everyone worshiping in one accord, all with the same heart towards God. Michelle Adams and Heather Bartos led the praise and worship, which was outside of some people's boxes. They combined hymns with newer praise and worship songs. Even now, I find it hard to describe the scene. Everyone sang all the songs with the same passion and in unity, along with the angels in Heaven. No one was divided because of what they were used to in their own churches. It was glorious!

People told me afterwards that the moment that they walked through the door of the church they sensed the Presence of God. That was what we wanted. That was what made all the difference... people who were hungry and thirsty to be in His presence.

In our bulletin, we didn't list any titles next to the names of the 14 pastors and lay people who came prepared to share. They were asked in advance to pray about bringing a word, scripture, and/or prayer—whatever God had put on their hearts.

Money for food was donated, and the people who gave it didn't want to be recognized at all. There was a lot of behind-the-scenes help that took place, and people didn't want any recognition for their parts. They wanted Jesus to get all the glory!

In light of the fact that the church didn't have any electricity or water, we had prayed about how to do a baptism there on the property following the service. God made a way by giving us favor with a local Amish family.

One day, Michelle Adams and I were leaving the church after praying, and we saw an Amish man walking on the side of the road. I asked her to quickly stop the car and turn around. We pulled up and asked the man if he might have anything that we could use to do a baptism at the special service that was coming up. He offered to let us borrow a horse trough, and it was perfect.

Message Shared at the Old Brick Church

What I discovered at the Historical Society of Whitehall[1]: During the time of the Second Great Awakening,

Methodist circuit riders traveled to this area and shared the Gospel in barns and homes. Lemuel Smith was sent to the Cambridge, NY, circuit and Samuel Wigton to the Champlain Circuit, which included Whitehall. They often came together in Hampton, NY, at the home of Samuel Bibbons who welcomed them and allowed them to speak.

In 1791, Samuel Wigton preached in East Whitehall for the first time; and by 1796, there were 10 Methodists who organized themselves into a Methodist society under Reverend Lorenzo Dow. Services were first held in various homes, but later they met in a frame building (barn) on the property located just west of the church. Later on, services were held in a local schoolhouse.

The lives of the circuit riders were very difficult... arduous. I found the following information on the United Methodist Church.org website.[2]

Typically, circuit riders traveled 200 to 500-mile routes on horseback, and at times, they preached every day. Sometimes circuits were so large that it took six weeks to complete a cycle. Exhaustion, illness, animal attacks, and unfriendly encounters were constant threats.

Freeborn Garrettson (who oversaw the circuit riders in the Whitehall area) *said this, 'I was pursued by the wicked, knocked down, and left almost dead on the highway, my face scarred and bleeding and then imprisoned.'*

Days and nights were spent in the elements, hunting or fishing for food and depending on the hospitality of strangers.

Theirs was a difficult and often short life. Prior to 1847, nearly half of Methodist circuit riding preachers died before the age of 30. But their passion for saving souls was unprecedented, both then and now.

In the early 1800s, through the famous preaching of Reverend Kellogg, Whitehall became known as an "evil and Godless place." At that time, the town was booming with many factories, and many activities were going on along the canal. It had many bars but not even a single church. But there were some wise and godly people who decided that a church needed to be built. So the first church, the Old Congregational Church, was built in what was then known as Skenesborough on the Burgoyne Road on the way to Castleton, VT.

In 1801, this area became part of the Brandon, VT, Circuit, which added a swing through the village of Whitehall. This circuit included Danby and Wells, VT, Granville with "Whitehell" and Crown Point, NY. (I suspect that the people who wrote this were familiar with the famous sermon by Reverend Kellogg.) In 1817, in Brandon, a great revival prevailed in town; and about the first of September 1835, a revival commenced and continued without interruption for some eight months.[3]

In 1826, the Old Brick Church building was built for $1,600; and during the years to follow, it became the center for Christian services and preaching. There are reports of revivals and meetings at which this little church was filled to capacity. Throughout the years, the Old Brick Church has changed very little.

All across NYS as well as in other parts of the country, the revivals that took place when Charles Finney rode into a town were remarkable. He preached about repentance and putting one's trust in Jesus; and God used him powerfully to bring people into His Kingdom. "Some historians called him the 'Father of modern revivalism,' and he paved the way for later revivalists like Dwight L. Moody, Billy Sunday, and Billy Graham."[4]

He was known as a "Walking Revival" and a "God Quake." Wouldn't you like to be known as a "Walking Revival," every place that you set your feet?

From January of 1826 through June 1831, Finney preached all over NYS; and because of his ministry, revival broke out. Many thousands of people became believers in Jesus during that time. There were parts of NYS that Finney termed "the burned-over districts," because spiritual awakening and revival had taken place so often in those areas that there were no more people left to witness to. For instance, in Oswego, there were reported to be at least 1,343 revivals between the years of 1825-1835.

Let's fast forward to 1876.... During the 100-year anniversary of our country and the time of the Third Great Awakening, there was a major revival that took place at the Old Brick Church in East Whitehall. The church held 250 people, but during the services, the church couldn't hold all the people who attended. Some had to sit outside and listen through open windows. Many people became believers in Jesus during that time.

I also found this Newspaper Clipping (approximately 1876): "The religious revival that has been going on at the First Baptist Church (in the village of Whitehall), under the guidance of C. C. Frost, has been fruitful of good works. Nearly two hundred people went forward and stayed for the inquiry meetings that were held after every service. The Baptist, Methodist, and Presbyterian societies worked shoulder to shoulder for two weeks of services. This is quoted as being 'one of the greatest religious revivals witnessed in this place.'"

In an article in *The Whitehall Times* from March 30, 1978 entitled, "The Whitehall Temperance Club—1876" (by Doris B. Morton, Town Historian), it was reported: "During the year 1876, a great revival movement swept Whitehall. All the churches held meetings and reported the many people who reformed as a result of the movement. This was true in neighboring communities as well. Speakers were imported to add to the work of the local clergy."

There was another article from 1878 that was found in an old scrapbook that read, "The religious revival is not at all in the wane at this place. Meetings are held during the week at the Presbyterian and Baptist Churches. At each of these places there is great awakening."

In 1883, revival broke out again at the Old Brick Church, and 40 more souls were saved; and in 1885, Rev. Joseph Zweifel ministered throughout the winter at the First Baptist Church, and 100 people became believers.

I'm sure that those believers were praying for the generations that were yet to come, praying for us. I believe that God was answering their prayers as we met to pray for our local community as well as the whole Northeast on Saturday, June 8, 2019.

T. H. Osborn

Some of you may be familiar with the famous evangelist, T. L. Osborn. Well, in 1904, another famous evangelist, T. H. Osborn (possibly an older relative of T. L Osborn), was brought to Whitehall by the village Methodist Episcopal Church for two weeks of revival services. There was a service every evening except on Saturdays.

The following is an article about this evangelist:

SPECIAL MEETING: EVANGELIST T. H. OSBORN of Chicago[5]... He is a fine speaker and singer and has marked success all over the North, having held meetings in some of our largest cities.... Bring a silver collection to help pay car fare and other expenses.

NOTE: Theodore Hollingsworth Osborn (1851-1932)
Osborn was known as "the Drummer Evangelist" and spent much of the late 19th century and early 20th century conducting religion revivals all over the country. They were usually in Methodist Episcopal Churches and often lasted for weeks. His religious exploits and successes were often mentioned in such periodicals as The Christian Advocate and Christian Workers Magazine. The August 18, 1897 issue of the Northwest Christian Advocate in Chicago stated, "Zeal, tact, and power characterize his work."

In 1991, the local Catholic church hosted an ecumenical prayer and hymn sing service, and other pastors from the area took part in the meeting. It was the third service in a series of meetings planned by the clergy of Whitehall. At that time, there were also many other special services where people from different denominations gathered together to worship and pray. This was just after the height of the Catholic Charismatic movement.

We can be encouraged by the fortitude and determination of the people of God who plowed the ground in our area as well as all across NYS. We must get out of our comfort zones, out of the four walls of our churches, and go out and reach the people. Don't think that it will always be comfortable; it wasn't always comfortable for the twelve disciples (most of whom laid down their lives for the sake of the Gospel), and it wasn't always comfortable for the circuit riders either. Jesus never said it would be comfortable, but He did give us the Great Commission which says: *And Jesus came and spoke to them, saying, "All authority has been given to Me in heaven and on earth. Go therefore and make disciples of all the nations, baptizing them in the name of the Father and of the Son and of the Holy Spirit, teaching them to observe all things that I have commanded you; and lo, I am with you always, even to the end of the age. Amen,"* Matthew 28:18-20 (NKJV)

My heart's desire is to spur you on to ACTION. It isn't enough to just believe it; you need to act on it. There are those for whom life and death hang in the balance. We believe that we are living in a season where there is great opportunity to minister to people in our local communities. There are many who are hurting, and they are just waiting for us to talk to them, to share the Good News of Jesus Christ. It doesn't have to be complicated or awkward. We don't have to be weird! We can just share the story of what Jesus has done in our own lives.

So, I ask you this: "What about God has changed from the late 1700s, the 1800s, and early 1900s?" The Bible says, "Jesus Christ is the same yesterday, today, and forever" (Hebrews 13:8). If this is true, and it is; then I want to ask you again: "Why not you? Why not me? Why not right now in our communities?"

I want to encourage each one of you to find out the history of what God has done in your city or town in days gone by. Stand on the Word of God, and believe that He wants to move in power again but in even greater measure than He has in the past.

I love what Charles Finney said. "Revival is a renewed conviction of sin and repentance, followed by an intense desire to live in obedience to God. It is giving up one's will to God in deep humility."

RESULTS

As a result of the prayer service in Whitehall, many people have been challenged and inspired to go back to their own cities and towns and find out what God has done in their communities. They have also been inspired to pray for the Northeast. Two women told me that they felt led to search out what God has done in their towns, and one of them who lives nearby found this information at the Pember Library in Granville, NY:

The Granville Sentinel – November 19, 1915

EVANGELIST SHELDON HOLDS FIRST REVIVAL MEETING AT BIG TABERNACLE[6]

Evangelist H. D. Sheldon arrived in Granville Wednesday evening accompanied by Mr. and Mrs. H. C. Mosher who have charge of the music in the meetings. Mr. Sheldon and his associates went directly to the Big Tabernacle on East Main Street and held the first service of Granville's revival campaign. The speaker held his audience in rapt attention and the intense interest manifested in his words and message give promise of great times in the splendid building provided by willing hands and loyal hearts.

The services are to continue for five weeks and at the end of that time it will no doubt be apparent that many who are today indifferent to the claims of God upon the life have found a Saviour, Friend, and Guide in the Christ of Calvary, and a church home whose spiritual help and counsel may be had continually. Special services will be announced from the platform and through the paper for young people, men only, women only and for the children and various organizations.

All the churches will unite in worship at the Tabernacle next Sunday morning when Mr. Sheldon will speak, 10:30 being the hour. The Sunday evening service will attract large crowds and those not wishing to stand will need to arrive early, although seats have been provided for 1,500 or more people.

In 1915, the village of Granville had approximately 3,600 people. As of the 2010 Census, the population had dropped to 2,543 people.[7] The fact that the organizers of these services were expecting over 1,500 people in a village that had 3,600 people was quite remarkable! That would be like expecting over 1,060 people today. That's REVIVAL!

I also have a friend who travels in full-time ministry throughout the United States. He was at the meeting at the Old Brick Church, and he took the details with him and shares them with other churches around the country. People who hear the story of what took place at this old church are excited and motivated to pursue similar responses from churches in their own communities.

God is surely on the move everywhere that there are people who are hungry and thirsty for more of Him.

On September 14, 2019, we held another regional prayer service that took place at our local recreation center (another neutral location), and we had 16 pastors in attendance, along with many lay people. God again moved in power, and we are looking forward to holding more prayer events with people from different denominations in our area in the future. One pastor who attended both services has since organized a weekly prayer service just for pastors.

WHAT CAN YOU DO TO HELP DIG UP OLD WELLS OF REVIVAL?

1. PRAY AND BE AVAILABLE

I want to encourage you to press in and pray for souls. The Word of God tells us that we should pray that the Lord of the harvest will send forth laborers into the harvest fields (Matthew 9:38, NKJV).

This is the conversation that took place between the LORD and the prophet Isaiah:

"Then I heard the voice of the LORD saying, 'Whom shall I send? And who will go for us?'

And I said, 'Here am I. Send me!'" Isaiah 6:8 (NKJV)

Are you willing, like Isaiah, to say, "Here I am. Send me!"? Are you willing to partner with God in whatever He calls you to do for His Kingdom right here and now?

2. FIND OUT THE HISTORY OF REVIVAL IN YOUR AREA

Where there has been revival in the past, there were people who were praying for future generations. There may have been many people who went before us who stood in the gap for you and me—this generation of believers.

You might want to consider finding out all that you can about what God has done in your area in the past. A good place to start would be your local library.

It is very encouraging to know that the people who were part of earlier moves of God were likely praying for us. Please use the information that you find to encourage people in your church, as well as people in other churches in your area, to believe God for an even greater move of His Spirit today.

CHAPTER 5

HINDRANCES AND HELPS TO SPIRITUAL AWAKENING

HINDRANCES

Many people don't realize that we have an enemy, Satan, who is out to render us powerless—to kill, steal, and destroy the plan of God for our lives. He does everything that he can to hinder the work that God wants to do in and through us on this planet. Sometimes people, often unwittingly, make his job easier by their complacency and lack of complete surrender to Jesus Christ and His ways.

DON'T HAVE REGULAR, ALONE TIME WITH THE LORD

Stay really busy so that you won't have time alone with the Lord and have opportunity to grow and mature in your walk with Him. Satan won't have to work very hard at keeping you from maturing, because you'll be doing that yourself.

Jesus was our example, and He spent large quantities of quality time with Father God. If we desire to do the things that Jesus did, we have to "do" the things that He did.

*So **He** (Jesus) **Himself often withdrew into the wilderness and prayed**.* Luke 5:16 (NKJV)

DON'T WALK IN LOVE

Walk independently, selfishly, not like God desires. You'll sound like a clanging gong and a resounding cymbal (1 Corinthians 13:1)! And you'll be a terrible witness, too.

I believe that it grieves the heart of God when His people don't walk in love towards each other and unbelievers. It doesn't mean that we have to agree on everything or that we agree with life choices that people make. What this means is that we choose to walk in love, treat people with respect, and show true care and concern about the needs of others.

In this the children of God and the children of the devil are manifest: Whoever does not practice righteousness is not of God, nor is he who does not love his brother. 1 John 3:10 (NKJV)

BE FULL OF PRIDE AND DON'T WALK IN UNITY WITH OTHER BELIEVERS

Act like you are better than other believers and that you don't need them. When you do this, you actually partner with the devil in doing his work of division. You may pridefully think that you're closer to God than other people, but in reality, you are deceiving yourself. A spiritually-prideful attitude is not from God.

Jesus said, *"Neither pray I for these alone, but for them also which shall believe on me through their word; That they all may be one; as thou, Father, art in me, and I in thee, that they also may be one in us: that the world may believe that thou hast sent me."* John 17:20-21 (KJV)

GET INTO VAIN DEBATES

Satan loves to see Christians become ensnared in disagreements and misunderstandings, and he loves to get them entangled in senseless debates. Be careful that you don't fall into this trap.

*But **avoid foolish disputes**, genealogies, contentions, and strivings about the law; **for they are unprofitable and useless**.* Titus 3:9 (NKJV)

BE CLOSE-MINDED TO OPERATING IN THE SUPERNATURAL THINGS OF THE SPIRIT OF GOD

"Religious" people will almost always come against a move of God.

*And **grieve not the Holy Spirit of God**, whereby ye are sealed unto the day of redemption.* Ephesians 4:30 (KJV)

Do not quench the Spirit. Do not despise prophecies. 1 Thessalonians 5:19-20 (NKJV)

God gave DUNAMIS power to His church. "Dunamis" is the Greek word, for the root word of our English word "dynamite." When we reject God's power, we reject Him. There are some people in the church who believe that the supernatural gifts of God are not for today. God's Word is always true. We have to be careful not to allow circumstances and situations that we've seen in our own lives to dictate the meaning of real Truth; the Word of God is the only standard. The Bible is always true.

DON'T BELIEVE THAT WHAT GOD SAID, HE'LL DO

*His mother saith unto the servants, "**Whatsoever he saith unto you, do it.**" John 2:5 (NKJV)*

*But let him ask in faith, with no doubting, **for he who doubts is like a wave of the sea driven and tossed by the wind**. For let not that man suppose that he will receive anything from the Lord; he is a double-minded man, unstable in all his ways.* James 1:6-8 (NKJV)

Find out what the Bible says about your situation, and believe that God will do what He said He'll do. Look for a promise, and believe that it is true and personal for you. Present your requests to God with thanksgiving (Philippians 4:6-7). Thank Him for hearing your prayers, and trust Him to work things out for good in your life. Be assured that He ALWAYS has your best interest on His mind, and He loves you like you're the only one He loves.

Let's determine in our hearts not to be unbelieving believers but rather to be sensitive to the Holy Spirit and be open to whatever God might want to do in all situations, even when it means stepping out of our comfort zones.

HELPS

GET TO KNOW GOD; CULTIVATE A PRIVATE, DEVOTIONAL TIME WITH THE LORD EVERY DAY

Get to know Him. Spend time in prayer; spend time worshiping Him; and spend time in the Word. When you do this, you'll learn to recognize His voice. As you get to know Him, His very nature, you will become stronger and stronger and be able to do the things that He has for you to do for Kingdom purposes.

*...but the people **who know their God** shall be strong, and carry out great exploits.* Daniel 11:32 (NKJV)

WALK IN LOVE TOWARDS ONE ANOTHER AND TOWARDS UNBELIEVERS

Christians are defined by the way that they love each other and the lost.

Some thought-provoking questions to ponder:

Is there evidence of the fruit of the spirit in your life? Do you operate in love, joy, peace, forbearance, kindness, goodness, faithfulness, gentleness and self-control? (Galatians 5:22-23)

Do you love like Jesus loved? Do you treat people the way that He did?

Are you moved with compassion, and do you genuinely care for people like Jesus did? Are you moved by the suffering of others and have a willingness to make a difference in their lives?

BE OPEN TO A MOVE OF THE SPIRIT OF GOD

Be careful not to allow fear or man-made traditions to stifle a move of God in your life and/or in your church. God wants to move among His people today in power, and we have to embrace what He's doing right now if we want to be a part of it.

It is important to be discerning, but sometimes people confuse discernment with their own fear of the unknown or their own reservations about certain things because of other situations that they've experienced or seen in the church in the past.

Keep in mind that whenever there is a genuine move of God, the enemy will come against it in every way that he can. He will often use unsaved people, broken people in the church, as well as those who are oppressed by him to make the move of God look false and to put doubts in people's minds about the validity of what's going on.

Let's just give God opportunity to move in our lives and our churches.

"There are four principles we need to maintain:
First, read the Word of God.
Second, consume the Word of God until it consumes you.
Third believe the Word of God.
Fourth, act on the Word."
Smith Wigglesworth

INTERCEDE ON BEHALF OF THE UNSAVED AND PRAY FOR BACKSLIDDEN BELIEVERS TO RETURN TO THEIR FIRST LOVE

Jesus taught us how to pray for unbelievers: *"Therefore PRAY the Lord of the harvest to send out laborers into His harvest."* Matthew 9:38 (NKJV)

UNSAVED SOULS are a priority to God! Are they a priority to you?

*For the Son of man is come **to seek and to save** that which was **lost**.* Luke 19:10 (KJV)

Jesus came to this planet on the greatest search and rescue mission that was ever undertaken. He came for each and every person who was ever conceived in their mother's womb, including you and me.

I love this quote by Dean Braxton: "God will go to every length possible, short of sin, to get every person to Heaven. He wants them there more than you do."

*The Lord is not slack concerning His promise, as some count slackness, but is longsuffering toward us, **not willing that any should perish but that all should come to repentance**.* 2 Peter 3:9 (NKJV)

*For this is good and acceptable in the sight of **God our Savior, who desires all men to be saved** and to come to the knowledge of the truth.* 1 Timothy 2:3-4 (NKJV)

God wants everybody to go to Heaven. Hell was created for satan and the demons, devils, and foul spirits. It wasn't created for mankind. We know that not every person will be in Heaven, but it isn't because God doesn't want them there. It is a result of their own free will.

Ask God to give you a burden for the lost....

This is a really thought-provoking quote by Leonard Ravenhill: "Can you remember the last time you didn't go to bed because people were dying without Christ?"[1] Now, that's what having a burden for the lost means!

As we read in Chapter 4, souls were of the utmost importance to the circuit-riding preachers of the 1700s and 1800s. I believe that these men of God should challenge us to be more in tune with the passionate heart of God for lost souls.

BACKSLIDDEN SOULS are priority to God! Are they a priority to you?

"Behold, I stand at the door and knock. If anyone hears My voice and opens the door, I will come in to him and dine with him, and he with Me." Revelation 3:20 (NKJV)

This scripture was written to the Church of Laodicea, to those who were Christians, not to unbelievers. God is concerned about those persons whose walk isn't right with Him, and we should be praying for and trying to help restore them to a right relationship with the Father.

GET OUT OF YOUR BOX, AND TAKE GOD AT HIS WORD

Even when the situations and circumstances that we see going on around us don't seem to make sense, we need to take God at His Word. His ways are high above our ways, and His thoughts are high above our thoughts (Isaiah 55:8-9). He sees the bigger picture from a heavenly perspective, and we merely see the smaller picture from a temporal perspective.

The Bible is our handbook for walking in faith and doing life on this planet. We need to read it, believe it, and "do" it!

CHAPTER 6

WALK IN YOUR CALLING AND FULFILL YOUR CALL

It has become even more clear to me as a result of the prayer event at the Old Brick Church, that part of the call on my life is building relationships with the people of God, especially leaders, and bringing them together in unity for prayer, worship, and ministry. We each have a call on our lives for Kingdom purposes while we're on this planet, and we need to find out what that call is and walk in it.

Believe it or not, before you were even born, God had already thought of you and had specific plans for your life (Jeremiah 29:11).

In Jeremiah 1:5, we see that the Word of the Lord came to Jeremiah saying: *"Before I formed you in the womb I knew you; Before you were born I sanctified you; I ordained you a prophet to the nations."* (NKJV)

You may know that some people have the call of God on their lives, but maybe you have wondered what God's specific purpose is for you here on this Earth. You may have asked yourself, "What is the call of God on my life?" or you may not have ever really thought too much about this before.

Do you know the answer to this question? It is partially your position in your family, but it goes far beyond that. Each one of us was born with a call on our lives, to make a difference for eternity. People don't realize just how important their calls are.

If our forefathers hadn't walked in their callings, God would have given their God-given purposes to others. He will find a way for His will to be accomplished on the Earth; however, He may need to do it differently than His first plan because we have free will. The choice is ours, whether or not to walk in our call. He won't force us.

Each of our lives is intertwined with many other people. If we look at every day as an opportunity to partner with God, then we will realize that God wants to use us to make a difference for His Kingdom.

God has a special and unique plan for your life. Are you willing to walk in it? You might ask, "What do I have to offer?"

And I will answer, "A willing and obedient heart."

*For you see your calling, brethren, that **not many wise according to the flesh, not many mighty, not many noble, are called**. But God has chosen the foolish things of the world to put to shame the wise, and God has chosen the weak things of the world to put to shame the things which are mighty; and the base things of the world and the things which are despised God has chosen, and the things which are not, to bring to nothing the things that are, that no flesh should glory in His presence. But of Him you are in Christ Jesus, who became for us wisdom from God—and righteousness and sanctification and redemption—that, as it is written, "He who glories, let him glory in the LORD."* 1 Corinthians 1:26-31 (NKJV)

"God does not call those who are equipped;
He equips those whom He has called."
Smith Wigglesworth

Chapter 7

What Might Revival And Awakening Look Like Today?

What did the early New Testament church of 2,000 years ago look like? In what ways was it different from the way that we "do" church today? If we take a look at how God moved in the past, we will have some clues to what might be missing in the church today. The end-time revival and awakening will be different from prior periods of revival and awakening, but it will have some common threads.

1. They were SPIRIT-LED believers.

*For as many as are **led by the Spirit of God**, they are the sons of God.* Romans 8:14 (KJV)

*"**My sheep hear My voice**, and I know them, and they follow Me."* John 10:27 (NKJV)

The Bible is clear that the children of God hear His voice and are led by the Holy Spirit. We learn to be led, and God will meet us right where we are if we submit to Him with willing and obedient hearts. As we learn to recognize God's voice through His Word and other ways that He reveals Himself to us, we will become more and more in tune with what He's saying.

2. They operated in the POWER of the HOLY SPIRIT.

*And the saying pleased the whole multitude. And they chose Stephen, a man **full of faith and the Holy Spirit**, and Philip, Prochorus, Nicanor, Timon, Parmenas, and Nicolas, a proselyte from Antioch,* Acts 6:5 (NKJV)

*For he was a good man (Barnabas), **full of the Holy Spirit and of faith**. And a great many people were added to the Lord.* Acts 11:24 (NKJV)

Are you operating in the power of the Holy Spirit? If not, why not? If fear is a factor, then determine to trust God so that He can bring you further in the plans that He has for you. He wants you to be full of the Holy Spirit and His power!

3. They shared the Gospel wherever they were—in the marketplace, on the streets, and at their workplaces.

Therefore he (Paul) *reasoned in the synagogue with the Jews and with the Gentile worshipers, and **in the marketplace daily** with those who happened to be there.* Acts 17:17 (NKJV)

We live in a society where many people feel that their religious beliefs are private, and some are very self-conscious about sharing anything to do with God in public places. God wants us to break out of that pattern of thinking and be freer about sharing Jesus wherever we go. Jesus said that the main reason that He was sending His Spirit was for us to have power to live right and to testify of Him.

4. They took care of widows and orphans AND fed and clothed the poor.

Sometimes taking care of the poor is looked at as being of lesser value than preaching or teaching, but God places very high value on taking care of those who are less fortunate. This is mentioned many times in the scriptures. For example, Stephen was a man who was FULL OF THE HOLY SPIRIT AND POWER, and he was chosen to help feed the widows (Acts 6:5). This wasn't looked upon as an unimportant ministry but one of great importance. Otherwise, the leaders could have just asked anyone do it.

When Paul and Barnabas were being sent off to minister to the Gentiles, this is what they were told: *All they asked was that we should continue to **remember the poor**, the very thing I had been eager to do all along.* Galatians 2:10 (NKJV)

Are you eager to remember the poor, or would you rather not be bothered with them? Do you look down on them, or do you offer them love, compassion, and respect?

*But **do not forget to do good and to share**, for with such sacrifices God is well pleased.* Hebrews 13:16 (NKJV)

*Pure religion and undefiled before God and the Father is this, **to visit the fatherless** (orphans) **and widows** in their affliction,* James 1:27 (KJV)

He who has pity on the poor lends to the Lord, and He will pay back what he has given. Proverbs 19:17 (NKJV)

Let's remember to watch out for those who are truly in need. When we do this, we show our love for God and for the people who He created, even the ones who sometimes seem hard to love.

5. They loved without limits, and those who were a part of the family of God were considered family.

*Therefore, as we have opportunity, let us do good to all, **especially to those who are of the household of faith**.* Galatians 6:10 (NKJV)

Here we're reminded to do good to everyone, but especially to show favor to our brothers and sisters in Christ. We should treat them very well.

6. All were called to evangelize.

THE GREAT COMMISSION

And Jesus came and spake unto them, saying, "All power is given unto me in heaven and in earth. Go ye therefore, and teach all nations, baptizing them in the name of the Father, and of the Son, and of the Holy Ghost: Teaching them to observe all things whatsoever I have commanded you: and, lo, I am with you always, even unto the end of the world. Amen." Matthew 28:18-20 (KJV)

You might say that this makes you feel uncomfortable or that this isn't your gift or calling. It is the calling of every believer to share the Good News of the Gospel of Jesus Christ. No one is exempt from this command. Some may operate in the gift/office of evangelist, but that doesn't mean that others aren't called to share the Gospel message. It doesn't have to be difficult or weird. You can simply ask God to lead, guide, and direct you as you share your story of what Jesus has done in your life with others.

And he gave some, apostles; and some, prophets; and some, evangelists; and some, pastors and teachers; **For the perfecting of the saints, for the work of the ministry, for the edifying of the body of Christ: Till we all come in the unity of the faith, and of the knowledge of the Son of God, unto a perfect man, unto the measure of the stature of the fullness of Christ:** *That we henceforth be no more children, tossed to and fro, and carried about with every wind of doctrine, by the sleight of men, and cunning craftiness, whereby they lie in wait to deceive; But speaking the truth in love,* **may grow up into him in all things,** *which is the head, even Christ: From whom the whole body fitly joined together and compacted by that which every joint supplieth, according to the effectual working in the measure of every part, maketh increase of the body unto the edifying of itself in love.* Ephesians 4:11-16 (KJV)

Jesus instated leadership gifts/offices in the church to help the people of God grow up and become mature—complete in Him so that they can do the work of the ministry (equipping the saints for works of ministry). Surely, sharing the Gospel was part of the work of the ministry.

7. They risked their lives for the cause of the Gospel.

Are you willing to risk your life to see people come into relationship with Jesus Christ?

...it seemed good to us, being assembled with one accord, to send chosen men to you with our beloved Barnabas and Paul, **men who have risked their lives for the name of our Lord Jesus Christ.** Acts 15:25-26 (NKJV)

8. Believers met together in homes on a regular basis, and they shared meals, took communion, had fellowship, and got to know one another personally.

*So continuing **daily** with one accord in the temple, and breaking bread from house to house, they ate their food with gladness and simplicity of heart, praising God and having favor with all the people. **And the Lord added to the church daily those who were being saved**.* Acts 2:46-47 (NKJV)

We have to make it a prime concern to spend time with other believers not just on Sunday morning but throughout the week. Our busy schedules make it difficult for us to be in fellowship the way that God desires. Some people even find it challenging to attend church even once a week. We have to make time to share meals, fellowship, and to worship and praise God together.

9. They walked in UNITY and SHARED WHAT THEY HAD with one another.

*Now **the multitude** of those who believed **were of one heart and one soul**; neither did anyone say that any of the things he possessed was his own, but they had all things in common.* Acts 4:32 (NKJV)

And all that believed were together and had all things common; Acts 2:44 (KJV).

But whoever has this world's goods, and sees his brother in need, and shuts up his heart from him, how does the love of God abide in him? My little children, let us not love in word, neither in tongue; but in deed and in truth. 1 John 3:17-18 (NKJV)

We live in a different culture than the one that the early New Testament believers lived in. The things that churches took care of back then have, in large part, been replaced by social programs in our society; however, we should still be mindful to be generous and share with others out of our own abundance.

At Out of the Box, we try to reach out to the poor and help meet their physical needs as well as their spiritual needs.

What does it profit, my brethren, if someone says he has faith but does not have works? Can faith save him? If a brother or sister is naked and destitute of daily food, and one of you says to them, "Depart in peace, be warmed and filled," but you do not give them the things which are needed for the body, what does it profit? James 2:14-16 (NKJV)

REVIVAL TODAY

We can be looking to build off of the original church foundations of 2,000 years ago, and we can be encouraged by the accounts of what took place and be believing God for even GREATER things. As we read what God did back then, we can allow our faith to rise; and we can be open to what He wants to do by the power of His Spirit today. He is Creator, and He is continually doing new things. Be reminded that things won't look exactly the same as they have in past moves of God, because He is continually doing something new.

CHAPTER 8

"TELL THEM THE TRUTH ABOUT HEALING" SPIRIT, SOUL, AND BODY

Therefore He is also able to save (sózó) *to the uttermost those who come to God through Him, since He always lives to make intercession for them.* Hebrews 7:25 (NKJV)

The *Strong's Concordance*[1] definition of the Greek word "sózó" is: to heal, preserve, and save. This same word is used throughout New Testament scriptures and refers to salvation, physical healing, and deliverance—all three.

While I was working on this book, I believe that I heard the Lord speak to me and say, "Tell them the truth about healing." Jesus came so that we could be healed to the "uttermost," whole and complete in Him in every area of our lives. He came to "save" our spirits, souls, and bodies. It is a package deal that He made accessible to us because of His blood that was shed when He took stripes on His back and then died on the cross at Calvary. Many people who are part of the Body of Christ understand that Jesus came to save our SPIRITS and to transform our SOULS, but few understand that He also made it possible for us to be complete in BODY as well, until the day that we go home to be with Him.

It has been my quest for many years to find out why the church today, as a whole, doesn't look very much like the early

New Testament Church. What is different, and what is lacking? It's as though the power has been drained from the church. This is primarily due to "whatsoever a MAN thinketh...." Stinking thinking is thinking that doesn't align itself with the Word of God. God wants us to think His thoughts, not earthly, temporal, or carnal thoughts.

Leonard Ravenhill is quoted as saying, "One of these days some simple soul will pick up the book of God, read it, and believe it. Then the rest of us will be embarrassed." I believe that in this hour there will be many of those "simple souls" that he was referring to.

The Bible says that God uses the simple things to confound those who think themselves wise in their own eyes (1 Corinthians 1:27).

From what I have observed, one of the reasons that people don't walk in the power of the Holy Spirit is that they don't take God at His Word. I think that this is why we see many more people healed in other parts of the world than we do in the United States (US). In the US, people will often automatically go to a doctor when something is wrong with them and then pray afterwards. In many other countries, people don't have this option, so they turn to God first.

People don't know how to handle it when they don't get the answers that they're praying for, so it is easier to lower their faith levels and expectation and make temporal explanations for their circumstances than to press in to God in faith, believing that He will do what He said He'll do.

Sometimes our own words condemn us. If we say we're believing for healing, but the words that are coming out of our mouths are words of fear, doubt, and unbelief, then we're really not walking in faith at all. We are actually being double-minded (James 1:6-8).

When we're not feeling well, doctors present the facts as they understand them, but we know that God is the only One who holds ultimate Truth. He is Truth. We need to come into agreement with the Word of God and speak words of life, healing, and restoration.

Sometimes we need to have our minds renewed by the washing of the Word. We may think that we're mighty men and women of faith, but a good reality check is to listen closely to what's coming out of our mouths most of the time. Are we proclaiming the same things outside of church that we're speaking to our friends at Sunday morning service or at Wednesday night Bible study, or do our words contradict each other? We need to ask God to reveal to us where we're really at on this topic.

Are we walking by faith on a daily basis or only on the days that we're with our Christian brothers and sisters? Let's be honest with ourselves and with God.

Do we really believe that God wants to heal people today, or do we merely hope that maybe He might heal just one person?

In the Old Testament (Hebrew), a similar word to sózó is rapha, which according to *Strong's Concordance* means to "cure, heal, repair—thoroughly make whole."

It's always God's will to heal people. In Hebrew, one of the names of God, Jehovah Rapha, means "The Lord Who Heals." By His very nature, He is our Healer; and not only by His nature, but it is WHO HE IS.

Surely He has borne our griefs (sicknesses/infirmities) *and carried our sorrows* (Pain and Sorrow: both physical and mental); *Yet we esteemed Him stricken, smitten by God, and afflicted. But He was wounded for our transgressions, He was bruised for our iniquities; The chastisement for our peace was upon Him, and by His stripes we are healed* (rapha). Isaiah 53:4-5 (NKJV)

We know that this scripture (Isaiah 53:4) relates to physical healing because it is referenced in Matthew 8 when Jesus cast out evil spirits and healed the sick.

We must continue to pray in faith for those who have diseases and are sick and believe that God wants them to be well. It doesn't matter how long someone has been dealing with an illness. God is outside of time, and He wants people to be whole in spirit, soul, and body.

He's a good Father, and He desires to give good gifts to His children. He wants us to be at peace and rest. He is our peace, and He wants us to walk in His peace every day, in every area of our lives.

After studying the Bible extensively, I have come to the conclusion that every word of it is Truth. God wants people to be well. He wants to SAVE them, deliver them, and heal them. He wants to bless people right now, right here on this planet, not just after their spirits leave their bodies; and He wants to use you and me to do this.

*Now to Him who is able to do exceedingly abundantly above all that we ask or think, **according to the power that works in us**,* Ephesians 3:20 (KJV)

God wants to give us fresh revelation of this truth: The same Spirit that raised Jesus from the dead lives in you and me. This is powerful, and if we can grab onto it, it will change our lives and the way that we minister to people. The same power that Jesus gave to the disciples (first to the twelve, then to the seventy-two, and then to all who believe) lives on the inside of you and me; and He wants to work through us to bring sózó healing to people—healing of spirit, soul, and body.

CHAPTER 9

HELPFUL SCRIPTURES TO MEMORIZE ON SALVATION, HEALING, AND DELIVERANCE

Daily, we need to think on these things and allow the Word of God to transform us from the inside out. We need to develop healthy habits that build up our spirit-man. If we do this, these living Words will transform our lives.

The Bible says that faith comes by hearing and hearing by the Word of God (Romans 10:17). In other words, the more that we truly listen to and read the Word, allow it to saturate our beings, and become part of who we are, the more we'll operate in faith.

POWERFUL, ENCOURAGING SCRIPTURES

Jesus Christ is the same yesterday, today, and forever. Hebrews 13:8 (NKJV)

For the eyes of the Lord run to and fro throughout the whole earth, to show Himself strong on behalf of those whose heart is loyal to Him. 2 Chronicles 16:9 (NKJV)

*"Behold, I am the LORD, the God of all flesh: is **there anything too hard for me**?"* Jeremiah 32:27 (KJV)

*"O Lord my God, I cried out to You, and **You healed me**."* Psalm 30:2 (NKJV)

*"For **I will restore health to you and heal you of your wounds**," says the Lord,* Jeremiah 30:17 (NKJV)

*"Beat your plowshares into swords and your pruninghooks into spears: **let the weak say, 'I am strong.'**"* Joel 3:10 (KJV)

"...I am come that they might have life, and that they might have it more abundantly (perissós)." John 10:10 (KJV)

According to *Strong's Concordance*, the word perissós means: superabundant (in quantity) or superior (in quality); by implication, excessive. Jesus came to give us abundant life.

*How God anointed **Jesus of Nazareth** with the Holy Ghost and with power: **who went about doing good, and healing all that were oppressed of the devil;** for God was with him.* Acts 10:38 (KJV)

*Inasmuch then as the children have partaken of flesh and blood, He Himself likewise shared in the same, that through death **He might destroy him who had the power of death, that is, the devil, and release those who through fear of death were all their lifetime subject to bondage**.* Hebrews 2:14-15 (NKJV)

*Surely **He has borne our griefs and carried our sorrows; and by His stripes we are healed**.* Isaiah 53:4-5 (NKJV)

*...that it might be fulfilled which was spoken by Isaiah the prophet, saying: "**He Himself took our infirmities and bore our sicknesses**."* Matthew 8:17 (NKJV)

*...who **Himself bore our sins in His own body on the tree**, that we, having died to sins, might live for righteousness—**by whose stripes you were healed**.* 1 Peter 2:24 (NKJV)
*"**Heal the sick, raise the dead, cleanse those who have leprosy, drive out demons**. Freely you have received; freely give."* Matthew 10:8 (NKJV)

*For this purpose the Son of God was manifested, **that He might destroy the works of the devil***. 1 John 3:8b (NKJV)

He came to undo all that the devil did do and still does.

Then JESUS went about ALL the cities and villages, <u>teaching</u> in their synagogues, <u>preaching</u> the gospel of the kingdom, and <u>healing</u> EVERY sickness and EVERY disease among the people. Matthew 9:35 (NKJV)

In these places, Jesus met people who came to Him in faith, and He healed them ALL.

*Beloved, **I wish above all things that thou mayest prosper and be in health, even as thy soul prospereth***. 3 John 1:2 (KJV)

This means that God wants us to be delivered, prosper, and walk in good health in our bodies and souls (mind, will, and emotions) as well as to have our spirits be whole.

*Is any sick among you? let him call for the elders of the church; and let them pray over him, anointing him with oil in the name of the LORD: And **the prayer of faith shall save the sick, and the LORD shall raise him up**; and if he have committed sins, they shall be forgiven him.* James 5:14-15 (KJV)

*...and great multitudes followed him, and **he healed** (sózó) **them all**;* Matthew 12:15 (KJV)

*But He was wounded for our transgressions, He was bruised for our iniquities; the chastisement for our peace was upon Him, and **by His stripes we are healed**.* Isaiah 53:5 (NKJV)

According to *Strong's Concordance*, the word for "healed" in this portion of scripture is "rapha," which means "thoroughly made whole."

Who forgiveth all thine iniquities; who healeth all thy diseases; Psalm 103:3 (KJV)

Verily, verily, I say unto you, "He that believeth on me, the works that I do shall he do also; and GREATER WORKS than these shall he do; because I go unto my Father. And whatsoever ye shall ask in my name, that will I do, that the Father may be glorified in the Son. If ye shall ask any thing in my name, I will do it." John 14:12-14 (KJV)

What are the GREATER WORKS? There are countless things that could be considered GREATER WORKS, including stepping off of a high-rise building and landing on your feet, seeing full limbs be restored on amputees, raising people from the dead who have already been cremated, and having no food in your house and later coming home to a house full of food. The possibilities are limitless. God wants us to come into an understanding that He is a limitless God. Imagine no natural, earthly laws of nature being barriers to God moving however He might desire to.

Sadly, I believe that people often limit God because of their unbelief. The Israelites limited Him, too.

*Yes, again and again they tempted God, and **limited the Holy One of Israel**.* Psalm 78:41 (NKJV)

*And **he sent them to preach the kingdom of God, and to heal the sick**. And he said unto them, "Take nothing for your journey, neither staves, nor scrip, neither bread, neither money; neither have two coats apiece. And whatsoever house ye enter into, there abide, and thence depart. And whosoever will not receive you, when ye go out of that city, shake off the very dust from your feet for a testimony against them." And they departed, and went through the towns, preaching the gospel, and healing everywhere.* Luke 9:2-6 (KJV)

*Grace and peace be multiplied to you in the knowledge of God and of Jesus our Lord, as **His divine power has given to us all things that pertain to life and godliness**, through the knowledge of Him who called us by glory and virtue,* 2 Peter 1:2-3 (NKJV)

In Jesus Christ and Him alone is found everything that we'll ever need for life and godliness on this planet.

PRAY IN FAITH, IN ACCORDANCE WITH THE WILL OF GOD

Find out what the Word of God says about your circumstances, and begin proclaiming the promises into your situation.

*And this is the confidence that we have in him, that, **if we ask any thing according to his will, he heareth us**:* 1 John 5:14 (KJV)

*"Again, truly I tell you that **if two of you on earth agree about anything they ask for, it will be done for them by my Father in heaven**."* Matthew 18:19 (KJV)

*"And these signs shall follow them that believe; **In my name shall they cast out devils; they shall speak with new tongues; They shall take up serpents; and if they drink any deadly thing, it shall not hurt them; they shall lay hands on the sick, and they shall recover**. So then after the LORD had spoken unto them, he was received up into heaven, and sat on the right hand of God. And **they went forth, and preached everywhere, the LORD working with them, and confirming the word with signs following**. Amen."* Mark 16:17-20 (KJV)

FAITH-FILLED WORDS ARE LIFE-GIVING WORDS

Be careful with your words. They can bring life, or they can bring death. Speak words of life!

Death and life are in the power of the tongue: and they that love it shall eat the fruit thereof. Proverbs 18:21 (KJV)

Words can bring life, healing, and restoration.

*"My son, **give attention to my words**; Incline your ear to my sayings. Do not let them depart from your eyes; Keep them in the midst of your heart; For **they are life to those who find them, and health to all their flesh.**"* Proverbs 4:20-22 (KJV)

Pleasant words are *as an honeycomb, sweet to the soul, and* ***health to the bones***. Proverbs 16:24 (KJV)

NEVER GIVE UP

Many are the afflictions of the righteous: but the LORD delivereth him out of them all. Psalm 34:19 (KJV)

If you hold onto Jesus and the promises in His Word, He will see you through any situation or circumstance that you will encounter in this life.

CHAPTER 10

CHALLENGING THOUGHTS AND QUESTIONS FOR CHURCH LEADERSHIP TO PRAY ABOUT AND CONSIDER

I believe that there will come a time when church leadership will have genuine care and concern for each other, when they will pray diligently for their communities and for one another, when they will let go of competition and become completely united in Spirit, and when pastors will exchange pulpits on occasion, without fear of losing people.

There are no denominations in Heaven, only children of God. In Heaven, we won't be asking people what church they attended. We'll be united in our worship of God and our love for Him and one another.

In an attempt to "protect" our flocks from errors in doctrine, sometimes we have alienated ourselves from other parts of the Body of Christ that we need. We all have something to contribute.

It is also possible that sometimes there are splits between people and churches, not because of doctrine, but because they have different calls. Sometimes the vision that one person or church has isn't the same vision that another has, and that's okay because God has different plans for each to do for His Kingdom. If we can just recognize this and not try to make everyone clones of ourselves, it will be very freeing for everyone, and God will be glorified.

When we had our prayer event in Whitehall in June of 2019, we were blessed to have believers from all different backgrounds join together in worship and prayer, and 14 of them shared words of encouragement. Each person who spoke brought an important piece of the puzzle concerning revival and awakening.

QUESTIONS TO PRAYERFULLY CONSIDER IF WE WANT TRUE REVIVAL AND AWAKENING IN OUR AREA

Do we genuinely care about the other pastors, church leadership, and congregations who are serving in our community?

Do we lift those pastors, leaders, and their congregations up in prayer on a regular basis?

Do we make it a priority to join them for special meetings and events at their churches and spend time in fellowship with them?

Do we include them in our invitations for special services and events at our church?

Do we encourage the people who attend our church to join together with other churches for outreach events in our community?

Do we have a superior attitude, thinking that our doctrine is more correct than others around us? (This is not referring to churches that are embracing blatant sin.)

Do we make decisions to speak up or not speak up about important issues in our churches based on finances and the people who donate large amounts of money?

Have we made decisions based on money rather than on what we believe the Holy Spirit has prompted us to do?

Have we allowed controlling people to speak louder than the voice of God in our church and in our lives?

Are we more local church oriented than Kingdom minded?

In an effort to be "seeker friendly" and "relevant," is our church neglecting to teach the deeper things of God to our mature congregants?

Do we honor and give older members of our congregation opportunities to mentor younger people?

Has the leadership in your church bowed to controlling people because they are afraid of losing people from their congregation?

Do we trust God to bring in and keep the people He wants in our local fellowships?

Are we sensitive to people who have vision problems (cataracts and night blindness), vertigo, autism, and seizure disorders with our lighting and choice of colors for backdrops?

Please pray about your answers to these questions and allow God to make the adjustments that He desires to within you. I believe He will speak to you and reveal what He wants to change in your heart, if you'll let Him. Be honest with Him. If you've answered any of these questions in such a way that you know there are things that aren't pleasing to Him, He isn't looking to condemn you for it but for you to repent and go forward with Him. We have important work to do for the Kingdom of God! There are many pre-Christians out there who need to come to know Jesus as Lord and Savior, and they are just waiting for us to reach out to them.

In Closing

I pray that this book has been thought provoking and challenging for you and that it will raise your level of faith and expectation regarding revival and awakening in this present hour that we're living in. There are many other things that I could have shared, but I believe that these are the things that God wants me to focus on right now... FOR SUCH A TIME AS THIS. May God bless you, prepare you, strengthen you, lead you, guide you, give you wisdom, and use you to help bring in the final harvest of souls in these last days in which we're living.

SALVATION PRAYER

If you don't already know Jesus as your Lord and Savior and you want to, please pray the following prayer from your heart to enter into a relationship with Him:

Dear Jesus,

I admit that I'm a sinner, and I need You. Thank you for dying on the cross in my place and taking my punishment. Please forgive me for my sins and come into my heart and be my Savior and my Lord. Please help me to live for You from this day forward. Thank you for making me part of Your family. In Jesus' Name, Amen.

If you prayed this prayer sincerely from your heart, you are now a child of God. You have just taken your first step in your journey with Him. Welcome to His family!

ACKNOWLEDGMENTS

MY SPIRITUAL PARENTS

Prophet Bill Emmons and his lovely wife, **Prophet Esther Emmons**

Reverend Timothy Bohley and his precious wife (my sweet friend), **Reverend Cindylee Bohley**

THOSE WHO SUPPORTED ME ON MY SPIRITUAL JOURNEY AND GAVE ME OPPORTUNITIES TO MINISTER

Reverend Jay Frances – for years of encouragement and always making time for me

Reverend Mike Benoit – for sowing into my life for many years

Reverend Mike Lemery – for trusting me with opportunities to minister, even when we were taking risks

Reverend Butch Race – for your friendship and for helping me with my Bible college courses (I love you, too, **Marcy!**)

Reverend Kevin Richardson – for encouraging me to go forward with my Bible college program. I would likely never have done it if it hadn't been for your encouraging words.

Reverend Jeff Hatfield – for welcoming our mission teams with open arms for the past ten years and for giving us an open invitation to minister at your church at any time

Reverend Jim Peterson – for taking me under your wing when I began ministering in Whitehall and for always having a word of encouragement for me

Reverend Bill Steinmetz – for teaching me some important administration skills and for giving me opportunities to minister in the pulpit

Reverends Peter and Lori Whitehouse – for your love and prayer support over the past several years

Nancy Insley – for praying me through a difficult time in my life

Reverend Yong Brierly – for your prayers, love, and ongoing support

THOSE WHO HAVE MADE "ROOM" FOR ME

Bob and Karen Weber, Bill and MaryLou Eddy, Peter and Marybeth LaFlamme, Dwane and Kari Hurlburt, Andre and Abby Wald, and Barbara Levesque

MY RIGHT-HAND HELPER

Laurie Donaldson – for all that you do to help the ministry run smoothly and for being a special friend

**TO ALL OF YOU WHO PRAY FOR ME EVERY DAY –
THERE ARE TOO MANY OF YOU TO LIST
INDIVIDUALLY, BUT YOU KNOW WHO YOU ARE.
THANK YOU!**

Especially my mother-in-law, **Barbara Merriman**, for

praying for me daily for years

PHOTOGRAPHER

Robbie Batchelor – for generously providing my photo

TWO SPECIAL FRIENDS AND MENTORS

Dr. Daniel Molloy – my boss for 20 years… You helped to
prepare me for the call of God on my life. You always treated
everyone with respect, and you always acted with integrity. I
watched you as you didn't show partiality to the person with
their PhD over the person who mowed the lawn or cleaned the
restrooms. I also appreciate how you patiently taught me many
administrative, computer, and clerical skills that I am now
using, even in the process of writing this book.

Last but not least, I want to thank **Reverend Dean Braxton**
for encouraging me to go forward with this book. Sometimes I
think that part of the reason you were sent back from Heaven
is to encourage me to fulfill my call on this planet. Every time
we have contact, you always given me an encouraging word to
keep moving forward with the call of God on my life.

BIBLIOGRAPHY

Chapter 1: BECOMING INTENTIONALLY UNCONVENTIONAL

1. https://banneroftruth.org/us/ (Quote used with written permission from "Banner of Truth Trust" on August 8, 2019.)

Chapter 2: REVIVAL AND AWAKENING – THE 100-YEAR PROPHECIES

1. https://greatawakening.blogspot.com/ (Used with written permission on June 27, 2019.)

Chapter 4: DIGGING UP LOCAL, OLD WELLS OF REVIVAL

1. Information in this chapter was taken from *The Whitehall Times* articles written by Doris A. Morton and compiled by Carol Greenough, newspaper clippings, scrap books, and misc. articles owned by the Historical Society of Whitehall, NY, unless otherwise noted.

2. www.umc.org – United Methodist Communication – Dale Patterson of the General Commission on Archives and History and Barbara Duffin of Barratt's Chapel – sources. (Used with written permission on June 27, 2019.)

3. History of Methodism in Brandon, By Rev. Bernice D. Adams, A.M.
From the *Vermont Historical Gazetteer*, Volume III, 1877, page 469 ff.
(Used with written permission on July 16, 2019, Brandon United Methodist Church, Vermont.)

4. Charles Grandison Finney19th Century Giant of American Revivalism: Christian History, Issue 20, (Carol Stream, IL: Christianity Today, Inc.) 1997 (Used with written permission by *Christianity Today Magazine* on August 8, 2019.)

5. Historic Lebanon, Ohio, Facebook Page. Article posted to Facebook page on 18, 2018 – *The Western Star,* Special Meeting: Evangelist T. H. Osborn, of Chicago will speak in the Baptist Church, June 18, 1903. (Used with written permission on August 13, 2019.)

6. Information found in archives at the Pember Library, Granville, NY – *The Granville Sentinel,* Evangelist Sheldon Holds First Revival Meeting at Big Tabernacle, November 19, 1915 (Printed courtesy of *Manchester Newspapers* in Granville, NY, by phone, John Manchester, on 7/18/2019.)

7. https://Population.us/ny/granville/.

CHAPTER 5: HINDRANCES AND HELPS TO SPIRITUAL AWAKENING

1. Used with written permission by David Ravenhill – October 10, 2019.

CHAPTER 8: "TELL THEM THE TRUTH ABOUT HEALING" SPIRIT, SOUL, AND BODY

1. http://www.eliyah.com/lexicon.html – *Strong's Concordance*, King James Version, John Strong, first published in 1890.